The
Little Box of
Inner Calm

Everything you need for a journey
toward spiritual awareness
and connecting to
your inner life

Christopher Titmuss

BARRON'S

A QUARTO BOOK

First edition for the United States and
Canada published in 1999 by Barron's
Educational Series, Inc.

All inquiries should be addressed to:
Barron's Educational Series, Inc.
250 Wireless Boulevard
Hauppauge, NY 11788
http://www.barronseduc.com

ISBN 0-7641-7303-0

Library of Congress Catalog Card
Number: 98-74961

QUAR.LBIC

This book was designed and produced by:

Quarto Publishing plc
The Old Brewery
6 Blundell Street
London N7 6BH

Project Editor: **Ulla Weinberg**
Art Editor: **Elizabeth Healey**
Copy Editor: **Alison Leach**
Designer: **Michelle Stamp**
Photographer: **Rosa Rodrigo**
Illustrator: **Chen-ling**
Picture researcher: **Laurent Boubounelle**

Art director: **Moira Clinch**
Publisher: **Piers Spence**

Manufactured by Regent Publishing
Services Ltd, Hong Kong
Printed by Leefung-Asco Printers Ltd, China

Contents

Introduction

It is never easy for us to comprehend fully the extent of what we are

We live in a world where we use tools for daily activities. We often forget that spiritual practices also provide tools.

Common to many of the world's major religions, these tools include art, bells, candles, and incense. In a rapidly changing world, these tools have remained largely unchanged for 2,000 to 3,000 years. As instruments for spiritual awareness, these resources have been passsed down from generation to generation. They are not gimmicks, but serve to remind us of what it means to be alive and conscious in the universe.

For generations, people have engaged in remarkably similar practices, exercises, and rituals to encourage such consciousness.

With the enclosed tools, this small book encourages readers to take steps on a wonderful journey toward a deep appreciation of all things spiritual in daily life. At the same time, the practices and tools will contribute to inner peace, an expanded perception and an acknowledgment of our profound interconnection with all of life.

A Buddhist monk in Thailand once told me that the whole earth was his temple. The sky was the roof, the earth was the floor, and the trees and mountains were the pillars of the temple. He had a wonderful sense of holiness as the center of life. He also said that humanity was the congregation and added that it was a pity so few people realize that we are all in the same congregation. His spiritual teacher commented:

"We are all **brothers** and **sisters** in birth, aging, pain, and death."

experiencing from one day to the next.

This small book serves as a basic introduction for prayer, meditation, reflection, ritual, and action in daily life. I have included a number of simple exercises and basic daily life practices. If you begin to apply these exercises in simple ways, they will encourage an inner renewal, deepen your awareness, and, I hope, inspire you to further explore spiritual teachings and practices.

The Tools

We have contact with the world
through our senses –
sight, hearing, smell, taste, and touch.
They serve as the doorway
that opens to let the world
into our heart.

We often take our senses for granted, forgetting how extraordinary it is to
have access to them. Each of the senses stands separate from the others, but
all find a meeting place within.

Here are **tools** for each of the senses, as well as a prayer for the heart, to
remind us that life is a spiritual experience as much as a human one. To
cultivate and develop each of the **tools** reminds us of the blessings of having
access to all the senses. Every one of the **tools** can contribute to inner
awakening and also

generate a whole new sense of
what it means to be alive.

The Eyes

We can develop a sense of calm and clarity
through our eyes. A beneficial aid to this is
the mandala, an integrated drawing
that reminds us of the vast web
of existence.

The inner life reveals

Seeing the Mandala

The **mandala** consists of a sensitive diagram
where all the lines are interwoven. Circles and
squares form the fabric of the diagram and by it
we understand that everything is interconnected,
woven together in one vast whole.

Through quiet and attentive concentration on the
mandala, we develop an inner energy that connects
with our heart and mind. The purpose of the
mandala is to help us witness life as a totality, an
integrated body of activities. **Mandalas** point to
the heart of things, the center of things from which
all diversity flows.

Many flowers, such as roses, reveal nature's mandala and we can make this mandala an object of meditation. We can also draw a mandala in vivid or simple colors, using a compass or round objects such as coins. In preparing the **mandala**, we draw mindfully, meditating with each movement of the hand. The outer edges of the mandala and the center embrace the whole.

The mandala reminds us that life has a spiritual connection by giving us a sense of wholeness. As we absorb the significance of the **mandala** into our inner life, we naturally begin to notice the unity of existence more and more.

The *perception* and *experience* of
the unity of all things
reduces *fear* and *anger*.

the outer life and the outer life reveals the inner life.

Exercise: *Make a mandala in a mindful and meditative way. Use the eyes to meditate on the mandala for 10–15 minutes on a regular basis.*

The Ears

The ringing of the bell is the signal of impermanence, the transitory nature of events and experiences. We usually ring the bell to start something or finish something.

Listening to the Bell

It reminds us to let go of notions of continuity, acting as a brake on the stream of consciousness. When we hear the **bell**, it interrupts our thoughts, preoccupations, and activities.

There are many occasions in daily life when we hear a **bell**: ringing from a church, or in the school playground, at a retreat or meditation center, during a ritual, or even the front door bell at home. Whenever we hear the **bell**, let us stop for a moment or two, be still, and reflect on the transient nature of all experiences, including our own lives.

Practice: *Use the small bell as a reminder of transience. Listen to the silence for a few moments after ringing the bell. Let us engage in the same practice when we hear different bells during our daily life.*

Deep awareness of the **bell** can help to break up a flow of unwelcome thoughts. The sound can help center us in the present moment and remind us to let go, to stop holding onto things. In the space after the bell has rung,

we **remain** *motionless, alert,* and *present* to that moment of life.

When the front door **bell** or the telephone rings, we stay still for three or four seconds before moving to respond. Those three or four seconds can stabilize the mind to a state of inner calm.

learning about the tools

11

The Nose

The act of lighting a stick of incense
matters as much as smelling
the incense when the aroma
wafts through the air.

Smelling Incense

We can make the lighting of the cone an act of reverence. We mindfully pick up the matches, strike the match against the flint on the box, and slowly bring the flame to the incense cone. When the cone is alight, we blow out the flame and place the cone in a safe, upright position. The gentle smell of **incense** will fill every corner of our room.

We can light the incense cone simply for the fragrance itself – or we can light the cone to make a profound acknowledgment of the mystery of life. Whether we have a religious or scientific view of existence seems less important than our relationship to life. The lighting of **incense** can express humility in terms of the mind's capacity to comprehend the wonder of life. Simple gestures of life can make a statement from the heart that our words fail to express.

In India, it is common for shopkeepers to start the new day of business by lighting a stick of **incense** in the doorway of their shops. Their purpose is to bring happiness and satisfaction to customers, staff, and all who enter the premises. It is a reminder to the shopkeepers that spiritual and business matters coexist when the heart is in the right place.

A woman in Asia holds a stick of incense. Her hands are joined together to give acknowledgment to the vast web of life.

Practice: *Mindfully and respectfully light a cone of incense. Sit in a meditative silence in the same room for 5–10 minutes. Be aware of the sense of smell and be reminded of the importance of the sense of the spiritual side of our lives.*

The Touch

Nearly all the major religions endorse the use of beads for prayer and meditation. Worry beads are also popular in Mediterranean countries.

Touching the Beads

We can use **beads** to recite a mantra in our native language. For example, we might say PEACE AND CLARITY, or BE HERE AND NOW, or ARISING AND PASSING. It is important to say the mantra slowly and mindfully.

Live

We recite one mantra or prayer for each bead so that the essential truth of the mantra or prayer begins to resonate deep in our being.

with

Love

The sense of touch is the primary sense employed with the beads. We are not in a hurry to say as many mantras as possible. In the Buddhist and Hindu tradition, there are often 84 or 108 beads. These two numbers represent infinity. In other words, there is no beginning or end to the circle of beads. Everything flows into everything else in the great process of life. As we move our fingers from one bead to another, we become aware of the end of contact with one bead. The death of that experience gives rise to the birth of the next experience: the contact with another bead. In the beginning there is the end and in the end there is the beginning.

Practice: *Recite one mantra or prayer for each bead for 10–20 minutes. Say the mantra consciously and slowly so the simple truth of it can be deeply absorbed.*

We can use our beads anywhere, at anytime. The beads provide the opportunity to develop both a calm and a clear understanding of the process of life. Mindfulness, respect, connection, transience, silence, and a spiritual atmosphere benefit our inner experience. In a real way, the beads can help us calm the mind, develop concentration, and experience the subtlety of connection through the fingers.

The Heart

It is easy to lose access to inner depth by becoming embroiled in day-to-day habits.

Reaching through Prayer

We might become very knowledgeable, very successful in conventional terms, but that success cannot fill a deep hole within us. We have only to indulge in a moment of madness, or see something go hopelessly wrong, and we realize how inept we are when dealing with the real world.

I wrote *Prayer of the Heart* to point the way to the deep issues of life. One of my favorite poems by the Chilean poet Pablo Neruda inspired me. The *Prayer of the Heart* can hang in a room or be framed and placed on a table or desk. My intention with this prayer is to remind us of the deep beauty of silence and stillness. If you wish, repeat the *Prayer* either silently or aloud so that the truth contained within it resonates within your heart.

To memorize a prayer or a statement of deep truth
can be a source of comfort during difficult times. I
have written one simple example of a prayer that
has meaning and significance for me – and I hope,
for you. You may wish to design and write your
own. We can write prayers and poetic reflections
for a variety of occasions. They act as a response to
the deeper intimations of our hearts. Such prayers
can become statements of universal truths that
apply to everyone who has ever lived on this Earth.

All of these practices and tools require a quiet
discipline. We strengthen the discipline when we
experience the benefit and joy in such practices.
We also commit ourselves to exploring the
mysteries of daily life.

Practice: *Read the* Prayer
of the Heart on a regular basis
so that its simple truth brings
calm to your being.

The Tongue

In certain traditions in the East taking
a cup of tea is a mindful ritual. The
purpose is to treat the ordinary
and everyday things of life with
respect and gratitude.

Taste the Moment

As a meditative ritual, we bring our presence
to bear on the whole process of taking **tea**.
This includes boiling the water, making the pot of
tea, pouring the tea, sipping slowly and gently, and,
finally, putting everything away afterwards. This
process helps us to slow down our mind, connect
with each moment, relax, and find inner peace.

We bring the cup slowly to our lips to sip the **tea**. We
then slowly return the cup to the table (or floor, if we
are sitting on the ground). We place our hands in our
lap until moving them again to lift the cup. We keep
the back straight. At the end of the ritual, we make a
quiet reflection to thank all who are connected to the
worldwide food chain.

Be mindful when drinking
tea, at any time of the day.
Even in the midst of a busy
café, we can practice the
tea-drinking ritual.

*Similarly, when eating, fully
taste or savor each bite of food.
Bring the attention back to the
simple act of tasting.*

Other Tools for Inner Calm

A candle generates a beautiful atmosphere of light, calm, and sensitivity. You can meditate using a lit candle. Sit 3–4 feet (1–1.2 m) or more from the candle, focusing on the flame. Be aware of the light from the candle, the flickering of the flame, and the burning of the wax.

To bring attention to a single candle can touch a deep place of quiet contentment within ourselves.

Reading is a meditation. We read slowly, receptive to the words on the page. A particular sentence, paragraph, or theme may touch us. We stop still to allow its truth to go deep within.

Music To make music a part of meditation, pay full attention to each note. Let the sounds pass through the air, into your ears, deep into your being. Let the music transform you. Become receptive to the extraordinary Symphony of Life.

learning about the tools

19

Reflection

Let
us find
time for quiet
reflection on
things.
We will not be in a hurry to think things
through. We will remember to be open,
allowing ourselves to look at situations in
fresh and unexpected ways. It is important
to pay respect to our potential,
to use thoughts skillfully for insight into things that
matter. Deep within our everyday mind, we can discover
a well of simple, unambiguous insights that flower like
a lotus on the still pond.

Importance of Reflection

If we gave as much care and attention
to our inner life as we do to
other matters, we would know
a different way of being
in the world.

We forget that the mind – including our feelings, perceptions, thoughts, and consciousness – is the instrument for experiencing and knowing the world.

Yet our mind often receives the least amount of our attention, although everything we do from birth to death involves our inner life.

The ancient injunction in the Buddhist tradition tells us to **AVOID EVIL** (intentionally causing suffering to others), **DO GOOD** (relieving suffering), and **PURIFY THE MIND**. These are three primary areas of reflection.

When the lotus flowers on top of the pond, it reminds us of our capacity to rise above issues and express something beautiful in life.

The key to the cleansing of the mind is awareness and reflection. **Reflection** opens the doors of perception, improving the quality of our life. If we have caused suffering, we **reflect** on the conditions that made us act in this way and what needs to change. We may realize that we also need the understanding of others to end the painful cycle of causing suffering.

Secondly, we **reflect** on ways to develop our kindness and compassion. We commit ourselves to acts of goodness. Thirdly, we practice purifying the mind. The combination of specific tools, good intentions, and regular practice will help purify the mind through the elimination of greed, hate, and self-delusion.

We need to make time to **reflect** on any manifestations of the ego. Do our work, home life, and social life mirror our intentions to live with a pure heart and clear mind? Do others matter as much as our family, our country, and ourselves? What would our family and friends say about our priorities? It is important that we stay true to our heart even if it brings misunderstanding from some loved ones.

Practice: *Take 15 minutes at least twice a week for reflection on overcoming evil, doing good, and purifying the mind. Resolve to develop as a human being. Beware of trying to justify unhealthy behavior.*

For many, Mary, the mother of Jesus, communicates the selfless love and purity of heart of a mother for her children.

23

How to Reflect and What to Reflect Upon

We are going through a difficult period.
We face uncertainty and know that there
is nothing that we can do. We don't want
to keep on thinking about it because we
end up only going around in circles.

Quiet Reflection

There is no specific technique for reflection, but we must have a firm intention to examine a situation in a fresh light, to find a different understanding of events. We will have to be very honest with ourselves. We might write down the benefits and limitations of something that matters. Sometimes we think incessantly. We often give ourselves a hard time, thinking too much about a problem. As soon as the problem ends, we want to immediately forget the issue. We easily neglect the opportunity to learn from the situation. As an example, imagine that we have had

Games and sports deserve reflection as well since we easily become caught up in either winning or losing.

Through quiet reflection or writing, we may uncover practical responses to find a resolution. If we cannot, then we may need the wise counsel of another, either a close friend or a professional. Sometimes a member of the family has a balanced and unprejudiced view of a situation. A good friend is someone who does not flatter us or automatically take our side, but who is willing to be honest and straightforward while supporting the friendship.

Conflict and negativity show the shadow of ourselves rather than allowing us to be bright, clear, and balanced in our views.

a bitter fight. We may notice the tendency to indulge in thoughts of revenge, or we may want to withdraw from that person in such a way as to hurt them. Let us ask ourselves:

What can I learn from this fight?

Can I let go of my tendency for revenge or withdrawal?

Can I let go of my tendency to attack myself for being misunderstood?

What contributed to this misunderstanding?

Does the painful memory of the argument have to dominate my perceptions of the person or of myself?

How can I demonstrate loving kindness, forgiveness, or equanimity?

learning about reflection

25

Developing a Capacity for Inner Listening

It isn't easy to listen to the voice within ourselves. Just as there are many voices around us telling us what to do, so the same experience can occur within ourselves.

The voice within

One inner voice tells us to do one thing, a second voice tells us to do another. Sometimes the voice is hard and sometimes the voice is soft. As a rule, we listen to the soft voice, avoiding any aggressive and reactive patterns.

Yet there are times when we need to make ourselves clear, to express a concern or a criticism.

It may not be easy

We mustn't forget that it takes practice. It is a skill to transform aggression into kindness, submissive behavior into speaking up for others or ourselves. We want others to listen and acknowledge what we have to say. We must be able to voice our concerns.

Sometimes we can hear our inner voice telling us we must make changes in our life. It is easy to ignore this inner voice. Others may tell us the same thing. It is easy to ignore them, too. We may need to take short practical steps, rather than trying to make a single leap from the known into the unknown. The clear signal of inner listening is that we do make worthwhile and practical changes in our life. One small, but deliberate step in the right direction is worthwhile. Authentic inner listening therefore becomes a liberating force.

We are naturally respectful when entering a temple. Let us be equally respectful when entering into a conversation with another.

We learn to listen to what is wise and skillful through immediate application of our priorities. Listening clearly inwardly does not necessarily guarantee satisfactory outcomes. There are many factors that affect results other than our honorable intentions.

to speak our mind.

We must be willing to experience difficult outcomes while keeping faith with inner listening.

Value and Limitations of Rituals

Rituals are not confined to religious matters. Anything can become a ritual. There is often a ritual in the way we start each day. Religious and other rituals have the potential to contribute to inner peace.

To use the tools for ritual, we establish a quiet, supportive environment. Your home will probably be its center. You might take a corner of the bedroom or living room, or use a table and set up a small shrine. You might use a plant, icon, small statue, or drawing to remind you of the importance of the spiritual.

I have reminders in every room in my home. In one room I keep a desert plant. It needs no soil. I give it only some warm water every few weeks. Then the leaves open right up in the space of an hour. It is a wonderful reminder of the resurgence of life, despite the most barren appearance.

I remember when I was in India staying in the home of the headmaster of a school in one of the hill stations. The master was a devotee of Mahatma Gandhi. Every morning this wise and saintly headmaster got up and went to one corner of his room and lit a candle and incense stick on his small altar. The altar contained a picture of Krishna, a copy of the sacred Hindu text, *The Bhavagad Gita*, a photo of Mahatma Gandhi, and a photo of his 90 year-old mother. When asked why he placed a photo of his mother on the altar, he replied:

"She represents for me love, generosity, and the immeasurable heart. My mother brings me closer to the Divine Mother of all things that many call Life."

A small statue of the Buddha can remind you of peace and equanimity, whether or not you consider yourself a Buddhist. We can devise our own religious rituals to give recognition to that which is greater than ourselves. Again, the resources of mandalas, bells, incense, and candles can create the right atmosphere for regular rituals.

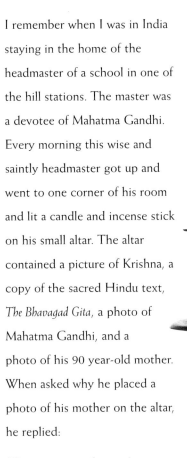

Meditation

Meditation brings awareness
and focuses attention on the
here and now. We become
mindful of the daily activities
of body, speech, and mind.
Through prayer, reflection,
and meditation, we deepen
our connection with life
from moment to moment.
Meditation helps us to
see things clearly, bringing
insights into issues of our everyday life.
It also touches places deep in our hearts.
Meditation should be at the center of daily
life. It is a natural resource that allows us
to experience joy, contentment, and
wisdom in the face of all kinds
of circumstances.

Meditation and Spiritual Practice

Spiritual practices and associated tools deepen
our knowledge of who we are. Practice is a key
word. It implies a day-to-day commitment to live
a conscious and caring life, supported by wisdom and
a profound sense of knowing what matters.
It is practice that makes the difference,
not setting lofty goals that
we cannot reach.

We practice letting go instead of blindly holding on.

We practice seeing impermanence rather than
clinging to continuity.

We practice giving rather than gaining.

We practice forgiveness rather than revenge.

We practice equanimity rather than reaction.

We practice speaking up rather
than living in fear.

We practice keeping noble
silence rather than being
self-righteous.

To live a **MINDFUL** life requires us to focus our attention on ordinary tasks. We start and finish a task as though we were doing it for the first time. We work **SENSITIVELY** and **DILIGENTLY**. Mindfulness in all tasks is a key feature of a spiritual practice. In such mindfulness, we pick things up and put them down in a gracious way. We move a houseplant with **LOVING TENDERNESS**. We open the door of our room more slowly and gently.

We make time to appreciate the relationship of forms and space in our room. We become more aware of light, color, temperature, sounds, and silence. This time is important to us. It conveys something intangible, but significant. Our heart and head do not overwhelm us. Conscious living and insights lead us onward, taking us deeply into the ultimate nature of things.

It is vital that we generate time to experience nature, to be in contact with color, the sense of space, and changing weather in the natural world.

learning about meditation

33

The Role of Prayer

Deeply religious people of all faiths
know the power of prayer.
It is also invaluable to be
aware of the intentions in
the heart behind prayer.

Acknowledge
the miracle of life

We say our prayers to remind us of our relationship to God. Prayer is the heart's response to the sense of the Immeasurable rather than just a belief in a personal Deity.

We can say our prayers at any time or location. Such regular prayers, often memorized, help to safeguard us from getting lost in the trials of daily life.

Prayer can deepen our humility teaching us to accept what is in store for us.

Spontaneous prayer comes from the depth of our being when we are faced with a crisis. We don't know what to do, or where to turn. The only comfort is prayer, which helps us surrender our will to a situation. Such prayers can help us weather the most difficult and wretched of storms.

The purpose of the Tibetan prayer wheel is to send prayers for peace and harmony in all directions.

Prayer emerges from appreciation and gratitude. The most ordinary details of life, the trivialities of daily existence, can spark a prayer of thanksgiving. We might even create a time in our life to write prayers of love and gratitude. In writing, we become receptive to a higher sense or dimension of things.

Prayers become one-sided when we are constantly asking for something. We then fail to acknowledge all that life has already given to us. True prayer also encourages us to be **GRATEFUL**, and to give, serve, and **OFFER OURSELVES** for the welfare and peace of mind of others.

Meditation with Mantra

In the section on the use of beads,
I referred briefly to the use of
mantra as a meditation. There
are two types of mantras.

One develops calmness, relaxing the brain and cultivating

inner peace. The second type of mantra offers those

benefits, but also has a devotional element. For example, a

favorite mantra of Buddhists is

Om Mani Padme Hum

which means Jewel in the Lotus. It shows a devotion to

the essence of the Buddha's teachings, namely

enlightenment. Some Hindus use the mantra

Hari Krishna or Hari OM

to show their love of Krishna (the Infinite). Some

Christians use the mantra Jesus in the Heart.

These mantras cultivate love and devotion for those with religious yearnings. We can practice a mantra silently, anywhere, at any time, with our eyes open or closed. We gently repeat the word or phrase so that it sinks to a deeper level. It is important that we do not rapidly repeat the mantra. The mantra helps to keep us focused, concentrating the mind, developing mental energy, and bringing inner calm.

It is important that we apply the benefits of the mantra in an ethical, caring, and worthwhile way. Otherwise the ego can use the extra calm and energy to manipulate circumstances for selfish reasons.

Practice *a mantra for 15–20 minutes a day to recharge the inner batteries.*

The Buddha is not for worship. Statues remind us of the importance of inner peace and facing the world with wisdom.

Meditation without Words

Meditation without words brings extra
benefits compared to meditation with
a mantra. The emphasis in meditation
without words is on inner peace,
clarity, and insight.

In meditation without words,
the mind awakens to the
profound significance of
awareness, silence, stillness,
and total presence. One way
to cultivate this meditation is
to remain completely still,
being receptive and totally
present to each moment.
Alternatively, we can use a
specific object (a candle, for
example) for such meditation.
Probably the most widely used
of all meditation practices is
mindfulness of breathing.

Like mantra meditation, we can practice
mindfulness of breathing anywhere and at any time.
A limitation of mantra meditation is that it can
become a habit, a word repeating itself over and
over in the mind. We can then repeat the mantra
without being in the present moment.

Mindfulness of breathing can be immensely
beneficial when dealing with pain in the body or
unexpected pressure upon the mind.

Practice: *Give 15–20 minutes per day to one or the other
kind of meditation. One continuous session is preferable. Make
either type of meditation the basis for developing inner calm.
Practice either of these meditations for a minimum of 21 days.
Then see the benefits of such a practice through your experience.*

Sit with an upright posture, then directly turn the attention to the breath. Be aware of **BREATHING** in and out. Experience the body expanding as you breathe in and contracting as you breathe out. Show particular care when exhaling when the mind may easily wander, drift, or daydream. There may be a few moments before the next in-breath comes. Remember to remain steady before the body draws in more air. If you are tired or restless, make the **BREATH** a little longer and deeper to let the air flow more freely. This releases more energy.

Sitting Meditation

Sitting in meditation is the finest of all resources available for calm and insight.

There are essentially three kinds of posture for meditation. We can sit **cross-legged**, we can **kneel** with the support of a wooden stool, or we can **sit** in an **upright** chair. It is important to remember the value of sitting with a straight back and neck. Tuck in the chin slightly, keep the eyes either open or closed, and allow the whole body to settle into the posture with an alert presence.

The two most popular times for formal meditation are morning and evening. It takes a certain discipline to remember to meditate daily. Once we establish a routine of regular meditation, it becomes much easier and more natural to us.

Mindfulness of Body is an important meditation for keeping us in touch with the bare actuality of physical life. We can experience the body as the interdependence of the four elements — earth, air, fire, and water — felt as firmness, lightness, warmth, and fluidity.

Practice *meditation to see the body as the interaction of elements. Sit in an upright posture. Be aware of the whole body, from the top of the head to the toes. Be aware of physical life as an expression of nature.*

Walking Meditation

We walk daily, to get from point A to point B. Sometimes it's a matter of a few steps, sometimes a matter of miles. Our mind tends to get caught up in where we are coming from or to where we are going.

Walking meditation is a specific practice we can develop at home, in the garden, or anywhere. We need 12–20 feet (4–6 m) for walking meditation. It can take two or three minutes to walk this distance.

Check that the body is upright, with one hand placed on the abdomen and the other hand placed on top. Then lift one foot up very slowly, moving it through the air so that the heel of one foot hardly goes in front of the toes of the other foot. Experience the foot touching the ground. When it is firmly on the ground, lift up the other foot, move it slowly through the air, and place it on the ground.

This meditation will ground you in the here and now, reminding you of the importance of taking one step at a time. As you develop this practice, you can apply walking meditation to your normal speed of walking. This will allow you to arrive at your destination feeling focused, calm, and ready for the next task.

Practice *for 15–45 minutes two or three times a week.*

Standing Meditation

We can apply standing meditation to a variety of situations, both indoors and outdoors: when waiting for a bus or train, standing in a line, or standing indoors as a practice.

In this meditation, **stand** with both feet close together — perhaps three or four inches apart. Place the hands on the abdomen. Keep the eyes open or closed. Experience the moment-to-moment contact of the feet with the ground and be aware of the whole body. **Stand** alert, to feel harmony between body and mind. I often have to take international flights to teach and lead retreats and workshops on meditation and awakening in daily life. Waiting for my luggage to come onto the carousel, I use this time as a wonderful opportunity for **standing** meditation.

Practice *standing meditation regularly, whenever there is the opportunity.*

Reclining Meditation

The reclining posture is obviously a very relaxing form of meditation.
It is not unusual to slip into sleep
during this meditation, which
may be what we need.

There is a certain tension that keeps the body relaxed
and the mind alert. When that dissolves, we drift
into sleep. The mattress, the direction in which
our bed faces, food and drink, and the quality of
our inner life can all affect sleep patterns.

Lie flat on your back with your heels together, or bend
your knees, drawing the heels up to the buttocks. Keep the
eyes closed. Use a small, firm cushion or even two or three
books to place under the head. Place the arms down the
side of the body, with the palms of the hands facing either
upward or downward. Let the whole body relax into the
posture. Focus your mind on your breathing.

*In the warmth of a summer's evening, we can
find inner contentment by stretching out on
the ground and being aware of all that
surrounds us.*

Practice for 15–45 minutes. If you tend to fall asleep in this meditation, keep your eyes open to avoid falling asleep.

We can practice this meditation at home, either on the floor or on the bed, and outside in the shade, on a summer's day or on a warm summer's night.

Daily Life

Reflection,
Prayer, and Meditation
have an enormous part to
play in our life, opening our
heart to love, happiness, and
understanding. These important
considerations must also help us
to live wisely in our daily life. It is
the combination of inner practices
and outer awareness that makes the difference.
This chapter addresses some of the important features of
everyday life.

What to Cultivate in Daily Life

There are three primary areas to cultivate in daily life for an insightful understanding: Awareness of Tasks, Expressions of Creativity, and Appreciation of Space.

Awareness, expression, appreciation

Most days of our life we have various tasks to accomplish. Sometimes we form long lists of these tasks in our mind. To connect with a task we pay attention to the activity. Stop regarding the task as a chore, or feeling resentful; practice approaching the task with awareness and respect. Develop the capacity to let go of some tasks. Learn to express creativity, and to make space for simple, undemanding enjoyments.

One father told me that he never had time for his children but felt he must tidy up before he could play with them. I told him to **REVERSE THE PRIORITY** and place playing with his children above neatness and order.

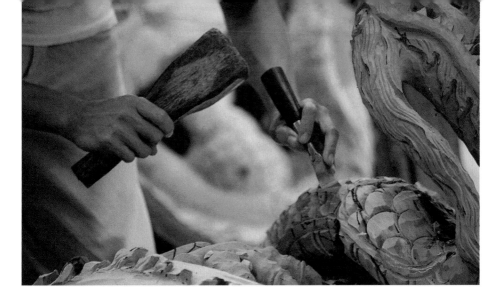

With so many tasks at home, we can lose the opportunity for creativity in daily life. Our mind might produce creative ideas, but unless tangibly expressed, these ideas are only fantasies lacking energy for expression.

Creativity becomes manifest through the body, for example through dance, t'ai chi, or yoga. Creativity becomes manifest through sound in singing, acting, and playing musical instruments, or through other arts in painting, writing, or cooking. There is something deeply nourishing about creativity. Yet, it can easily get neglected when we let ourselves become preoccupied with daily detail.

After a full day involving meetings, conversations, and time-filling activities we are often content to have some space to be alone. The element of space is important for inner calm. It is important to recognize space in daily life.

We learn to appreciate the space between what we see and what we hear. We appreciate the space in the sky above and views around. We try to find a balance in our home. When there is a strong sense of space thoughts do not clutter our mind. We can appreciate the space around the body, the space between thoughts, and the benefits of a spacious and accommodating mind.

Intention, Action, Result

The threefold awareness for daily life
embraces intention, action, and result.
Each one of these matters a great deal.

Threefold awareness

Living wisely

We can learn much about ourselves through **intention**, **action**, and **result**. If we slip back, then we try again — that is the challenge. We live wisely by staying in touch with each of these three important features. If we see that our actions are unskillful, our practice gives us the strength to make changes in our life.

Chess is a game of skill. It needs to be appreciated as such so that we can respect the winning skill of another as much as our own.

One important area in this threefold process is keeping faith with our determination to follow things through. Commitments require interest, determination, and the willingness to sustain our focus. This means that at times we have hurdles to overcome. It is worth giving regular consideration to our relationship to the threefold awareness.

Keeping a journal can be a useful tool for knowing ourselves or for considering changes we wish to make. Be aware of three considerations:

1. *The benefits of change*
2. *The disadvantages of not making changes*
3. *Practical steps to take, starting today*

We need to bring a *meditative awareness* to the list. We might take a walk before completing it.

helps to free the mind from the problems or addictions of the past.

We need to remember that what happens in our inner life manifests itself outwardly.

If there is greed, hate, and confusion inwardly, it will show itself outwardly. If there is generosity, love, and creativity, it will also manifest itself through our activities. Working with our inner life contributes to the fullness of life. Many hours of our life may be involved in a particular activity such as study, work, job-hunting, or parenting. We need to be aware of the primary **intention**, the quality of the **action**, and the relationship that we have to **results**. If we bear in mind all three, then we can find inner peace while living a full life.

Do our actions harm others and ourselves?
What are the benefits for others and us?

Relationship to Results

Results matter. We may like to think
that results are in our hands.
This view becomes exaggerated
when we have an inflated sense
of self-importance.

Results matter

At times, it can seem as if
or even two steps

It is worth remembering that many

factors contribute to the outcome

of our intentions and actions. Clinging to **results**

can lead to anguish and feelings of failure or

reinforce the judgmental mind. Succeeding can

inflate the ego, which can lead to gross ambition, or

intolerance, and cause us to lose touch with others.

It takes practical steps to find a depth of inner calm

and peace of mind. It takes wisdom to deal with daily

circumstances. I do not mean to say that life becomes

easier and easier. Many events in life can have a sudden

and unexpected impact upon us.

Yet we keep developing our practices and use the tools that support inner development as a human being.

Sometimes we do not have the necessary resources, skills, or aptitude to deal with or understand what goes on within us. It is important to be honest with ourselves about this. Addictions, painful memories, lack of self worth, rage, and conflict may require the wise and skilled counsel of others. We must acknowledge this. We must seek out support. We should not deceive ourselves into thinking we can solve all our problems.

Reflections, prayers, and meditation may open up our inner life in wonderful ways by exposing us to extraordinary experiences. We may not have the insights to understand the depth or significance of such experiences. This book contributes to finding wisdom in daily life. Obviously, it cannot provide all the answers to every concern. I believe it will point you in the right direction. The practices applied on a regular basis will contribute in a healthy way to daily life.

We take two steps forward and one step back, forward and three steps back.

Body, Speech, and Mind

A woman attended a retreat with me at a monastery in Majorca. Later, driving one night on a winding mountain road, she suddenly saw a sheep in the path of her car.

Staying calm

She turned her steering wheel sharply to avoid it and the car hit a cliff. She was stuck in the dark on a lonely road and had to wait hours for another vehicle to come by. She told me that at that moment she remembered some words I had said:

"Every moment of practice will be worth its

She told me that she stayed calm and relaxed and dealt with the situation. Her experience reminds us all of the importance of practicing to stay focused. We mindfully breathe in and out to stay steady in the face of difficult situations that easily affect body, speech, and mind.

We can practice for mindfulness of the **body** in a variety of situations for one week. Are we in touch with the **body**, out of touch with it, taking it for granted, or worrying over it? Do we pay attention to diet, exercise, and posture? Can we experience the **body** as an expression of nature, made up of genetic material, rather than as a personal possession?

weight in gold at times when something unexpected happens."

We can practice mindfulness of **speech** for one week. Take notice of the words we use, the attitude that we adopt, and the tone of our voice. Make a commitment to speaking about others in a way that we would wish others to speak about us.

We can practice awareness of states of **mind** for one week. We observe the states of **mind** coming and going and do not cling to them. We learn to express healthy states of **mind** and practice learning from problematical **mind** states.

Resolutions

There is something important to
remember when we are making
resolutions. We must apply the
resolution as close as possible
to the moment of making it.

Supportive environments

The further in time we are from applying the **resolution**, the less likely we are to initiate it. Our **resolve** may be to stop doing something – for example, smoking, eating desserts, complaining, or neglecting our children. Alternatively, our resolve may be to start something — for example, regular exercise, vegetarian diet, or acts of kindness.

It can be useful to make a clear announcement to our family and friends of our **resolution** so that they can support it. We can also make a written statement of the **resolution** and read it out aloud every day. We can avoid places of temptation — shops, bars, bakeries — and place ourselves in supportive environments — the park, gym, vegetarian restaurants, and on the carpet with the kids.

It is easy to lose heart if we slip back from our **resolve**. We have to prepare for that, picking ourselves up again to carry on. A key feature of making a **resolution** is daily effort.

Worship and Everyday Environment

It used to be said that cleanliness is next to Godliness. Today we might say that calmness is next to Godliness.

For some, the

This book will benefit all of us, whether we have a religious belief or not. We may find that the practices and guidelines in this book shed a helpful light on our religious beliefs, bringing God closer to us. Or we may find greater trust and confidence in the path toward enlightening our life.

We can find the strength to draw upon a wide variety of resources, near and far. We may consider using places of religious **worship**, such as churches and temples, for our practice. Some places of **worship** embrace centuries of silence, which can be felt in the atmosphere. There may be an old church or temple near our office or college that is suitable for spending short periods of time. Such places are often open during the day or evenings and it is usually easy to find a quiet corner for reflection and meditation.

Such environments give support in times of difficulty such as unexpected change, loss, separation, and pain. We may feel that it is not necessary to adopt a fixed set of religious beliefs that conflict with others' religious and secular beliefs. Instead, we can develop a deep respect for life, treating all life with reverence, engaging in noble actions, meditating, and listening to wisdom.

We can acknowledge the unfolding process of life and the deep experience of the interconnection of all things. Through such commitments and dedications, we pay respect to ourselves, and to the important features of all religions and worthwhile philosophies of life.

park or anywhere in nature can be a temple.

Fulfillment

The intention of this book is to serve as a practical introduction to our inner life.

Every moment matters.

Every act counts.

Some think it is rather selfish and egotistical to give time to reflection, prayer, and meditation. This is a misunderstanding. Inner peace, a loving heart, and a clear mind benefit others near and far. Our personal relationships, livelihoods, and values all reflect a depth of understanding.

There is a natural sharing of our wisdom that comes via body, speech, and mind. It is the expansion of the heart that speaks, not the self-righteousness of the mind.

Our practices help us, no matter who we are, to deal with our many challenges. We can look directly at the tiger and see that it has no teeth. We have a wonderful potential to transform our life. By opening up the doors of perception, we can know profound experiences while engaging in day-to-day activities. This means a whole new way of being in the world.

We are not indifferent and casual about life, nor are we in a desperate hurry to achieve personal ambitions. We know a middle ground that is wise and skillful. We understand that the true riches of life are found within ourselves. Wealth, property, and status are no substitute.

May all beings live mindfully.
May all beings live wisely.
May all beings know an enlightened life.

GENUINE FULFILLMENT EMBRACES EVERY FEATURE OF OUR REMARKABLE EXISTENCE FROM BIRTH TO DEATH. WE HAVE THE POTENTIAL TO KNOW AN ENLIGHTENED AND LIBERATED LIFE. LET US FULFILL THIS POTENTIAL.

learning about daily life

63

Index

Credits

The author would like to express gratitude to the Buddha, Venerable Ajahn Dhammadharo and the late Venerable Ajahn Buddhadasa of Thailand throughout my six years as a Buddhist monk. My gratitude also goes to Sharda Rogell and Gill Farrer-Halls for their editing skills. I also wish to thank my daughter, Nshorna, Gwanwyn Williams, my mother and late father.

For more information, write to: Gaia House, West Ogwell, near Newton Abbot, Devon, TQ12 6EN, United Kingdom. Tel: 44 (0) 1626 333613 Fax: 44 (0) 1626 352650 e-mail: gaiahouse@gn.apc.org or insightmeditation@gn.apc.org website: http://www.gn.apc.org/gaiahouse or http://www.insightmeditation.org

Quarto would like to thank the following for providing pictures reproduced in this book:

The Bridgeman Art Library 8bl; **Crucial Books/Alun Jones** 13, 17r, 22bl, 27br, 28bl, 33, 35tl, 40l, 43l, 51, 55, 57, 58, 60/61; **Flowers & Foliage/Rachel Lever** 39l; **The Image Bank** 11l, 16bl, 35bl, 37cl, 44r, 63

All other photographs are copyright of Quarto Publishing plc.

Christopher Titmuss, co-founder of Gaia House, teaches awakening and insight meditation world-wide. He is the author of *The Power of Meditation* and *Light on Enlightenment*.